BENJI'S MESSY ROOM

Diane N. Quintana
& Jonda S. Beattie

Copyright © 2022 Release Repurpose Reorganize LLC

All rights reserved. No part of this publication may be reproduced, distributed, or transmitted in any form or by any means, including photocopying, recording, or other electronic or mechanical methods, without the prior written permission of the publisher, except in the case of brief quotations embodied in critical reviews and certain other noncommercial uses permitted by copyright law. For permission requests, write to the publisher at the address below.

ISBN 978-1-7359684-3-8

Printed in the United States of America

ReleaseRepurpose.com

My name is Benji.
I am five years old.

This is my family.

I have a mother, a father, and an older sister, Heather.

Heather is eight years old.

This is my room.

I have lots of fun playing in my room.

Sometimes I have so much fun that all my toys, puzzles, books, dinosaurs, and stuffed animals get mixed up together.

What do I do when my mother asks me to pick up my room?

I stand outside my room, make fists, stomp my feet, and make a face.

I don't WANT to pick up my room. The mess is too big!

But what do I do when my mother asks me to pick up my shoes and my dirty clothes?

I play the "seek and sort" game.
I find my shoes, match the pairs, and put them in my closet.

Then I find all my dirty clothes and put them in the laundry basket.

What do I do when my mother asks me to pick up my books?

I find my books from
all over my room.

Some are even under my bed.

I put all the books
on my bookshelf.

What do I do when my mother asks me to pick up my blocks?

My blocks are scattered all over my room.

I look for the biggest blocks first and stack them on the toy shelf.

Then I find the next biggest building blocks and stack them on the toy shelf too.

I keep doing this until I have all the building blocks picked up.

What do I do when my mother asks me to pick up my puzzles?

I find my puzzle boards and match up their pieces.

Then I put them on my toy shelf.

What do I do when my mother asks me to pick up my dinosaurs and stuffed animals?

I find my stuffed animals and dinosaurs and toss them up into the hammock.

What do I do when my mother asks me to pick up my Legos®?

I take the bin that the Legos® belong in and crawl along the floor, picking up all the little Legos® pieces as I go.

Then I put the bin back on the toy shelf.

What do I do when my mother asks me to pick up my army men?

I take the bin that the army men belong in with me as I play search and rescue to put the army men back where they belong in the bin.

Then I put the bin back on the toy shelf.

What do I do when my mother asks me to pick up my cars and trucks?

I find the cars and trucks bin and put it on the floor.

Then I push my cars from all over the room to where I put the bin.

Some of them won't fit in the bin.

I put the bin full of cars and trucks away.

Then I line up the extras on the floor.

What do I do when my mother says, "I think you have too many cars and trucks now.

Why don't you pick out ten to give to some other children who may not have so many cars and trucks?"

This makes me sad.

I like ALL my cars and trucks.

I don't want to give any away.

My mother shows me that I have two or three of some cars.

I ask my mother if I can only give away the ones that are the same as the ones I already have.

My mother smiles and says, "Yes!"

My mother brings me a box.

I sort through my cars and trucks and put the ones that I have two of in the box.

Now all my cars and trucks fit in their bin.

What do I do when my mother says, "You have done such a wonderful job picking up your room!

Would you like to meet a friend at the indoor playground this afternoon?"

I laugh and say, "Yes!"

NOTE TO PARENTS

This book was written for parents and children to share.

The authors took some basic organizational strategies:
- Break projects down into small manageable steps
- Sort like with like
- Cull collections
- Assign a place or a home for belongings
- Reward for jobs completed

The authors then applied these strategies to the common task of picking up a room.

People are often overwhelmed when given what to them seems like a large project. The first step is to break the project down into small manageable steps.

Study the illustrations. Notice that Benji did not do a perfect job. You will notice that the bookshelf is a bit untidy, and a sock is hanging out of the laundry basket. Still, Benji did a great job for his age, and his efforts are accepted and praised.

We encourage parents to accept the organizing job done by their child so as not to minimize the child's efforts.

There is also a reward for completing the task. As professional organizers, the authors encourage their clients to reward themselves when a project is complete. Rewarding Benji shows appreciation for his effort.

OTHER BOOKS FOR CHILDREN BY DIANE AND JONDA

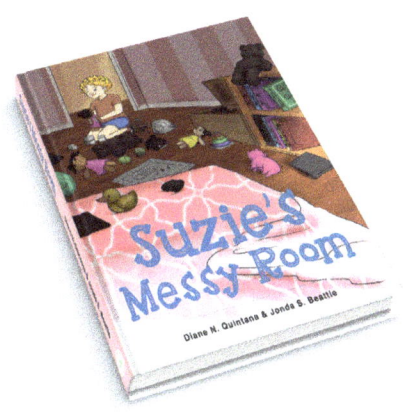

Suzie's Messy Room by Diane N. Quintana and Jonda S. Beattie

Suzie is a typical, active five-year-old little girl. She loves playing with all her toys in her room and sometimes creates a real mess! When her mother asks her to pick up her room, Suzie is overwhelmed and doesn't know how to begin. Suzie's mother helps her complete the job by breaking the project into small tasks that Suzie is able to finish easily. Doing this teaches Suzie how to get organized. Basic principles of organizing included in this story:

- Break projects down into small steps
- Sort like with like
- Cull collections
- All belongings need a home
- Reward for completed tasks

OTHER BOOKS BY DIANE AND JONDA

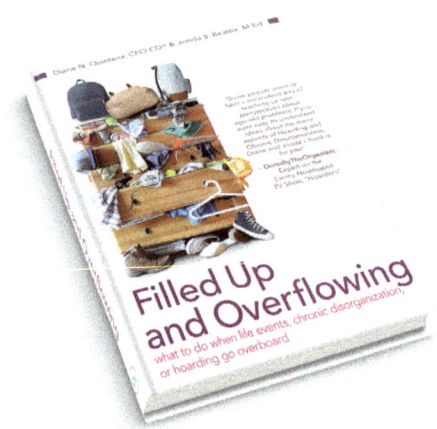

Filled Up & Overflowing was written to help you and your family members, friends, and spouses find answers to questions and concerns about the safety and comfort of their loved one in their space.

ABOUT THE AUTHORS

Diane N. Quintana is a Certified Professional Organizer® through the National Association of Productivity and Organizing Professionals (NAPO) and a Certified Professional Organizer in Chronic Disorganization® through the Institute for Challenging Disorganization (ICD®). She is also a presenter and best-selling author.

Diane N. Quintana is a former elementary school teacher. She is the owner of DNQ Solutions, LLC a professional organizing company in Metro-Atlanta that works with both residential and small business clients.

Jonda S. Beattie is a professional organizer, presenter, and best-selling author.

Jonda S. Beattie is a former elementary special education teacher and a former lead teacher of special education with a master's degree in special education. She is the owner of Time Space Organization a professional organizing company in Metro-Atlanta that works with both residential and small business clients.

Both Diane and Jonda are active members of NAPO, NAPO-Georgia, and ICD®.

In 2020, Diane and Jonda founded Release Repurpose Reorganize, LLC. Their vision for working together is: To empower you to cultivate better health, better relationships, and a better lifestyle.

Our mission is to guide you to build your refuge in the world. To release, repurpose and reorganize what you own so it serves you instead of you serving it.

ORGANIZE YOUR HOME 10 MINUTES AT A TIME DECK OF CARDS

Parents: use this deck of cards to help you organize your home in short 10-minute segments of time.

These positive cards will motivate you to declutter, organize and simplify your stuff.

Each of the colorful 50 cards outlines 4 – 6 simple steps to organize and accomplish 1 task in a 10-minute time span.

An added benefit is that you can involve your children as some of the cards are labeled Child-Friendly.

All you do is pick a card from the deck, follow the step-by-step instructions, and you are done in 10 minutes or less.

Easy peasy!

This deck of cards is made in the USA and available to purchase at:
www.releaserepurpose.com/organizingtools

HOME SOLUTIONS COURSE

The Home Solutions Course begins with The Basics. This course is for the person who would like to do it on their own but wants some guidance.

The Basics module sets the stage and gives you basic information you can apply to almost every area of your home.

If you want more detailed information, instruction, and ideas for organizing specific areas within your home check out the following modules:

Organize Your Bedroom

Organize the Bathroom

Organize the Closet

Organize the Kitchen and pantry

Organize the Home Office and Paperwork

Organize the Laundry

Organize the Family Room/Dining Table

Organize the Children's Room

Organize the Garage, Carport, Shed House

This course (**The Basics**) and the modules listed above
are available for purchase on our website:

https://releaserepurpose.com/organizingtools

www.ingramcontent.com/pod-product-compliance
Lightning Source LLC
Chambersburg PA
CBHW051318110526
44590CB00031B/4391